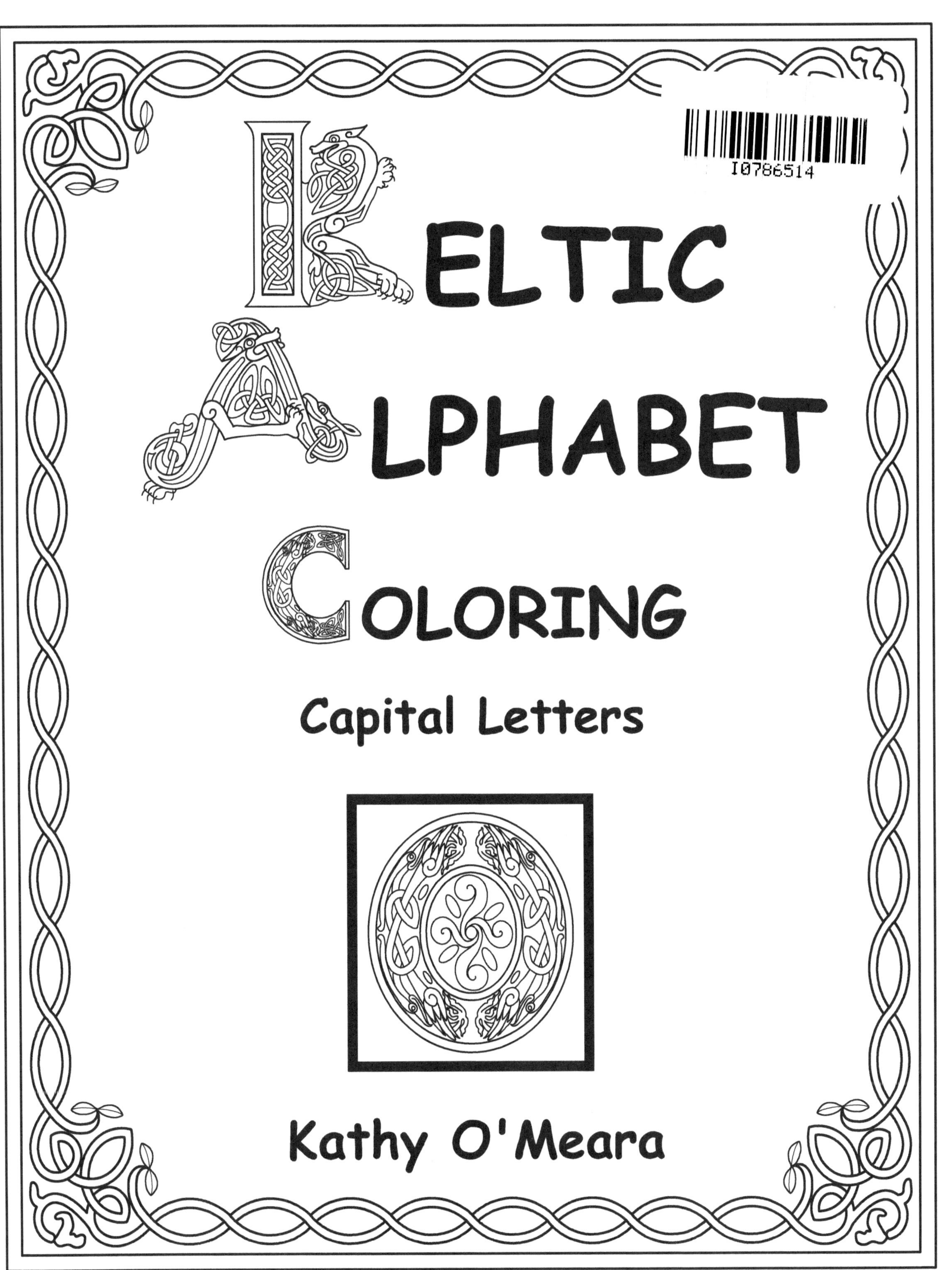

KELTIC
ALPHABET
COLORING
Capital Letters
Kathy O'Meara

Perelandra
Design

This book is dedicated
to my Mother, Johanna O'Meara,
and her "Friend" Dirk, who provided support
and encouragement through long hot summers
as I sat in front of my air conditioner
and designed these pages.

<u>Other Books by Kathy O'Meara</u>
Keltic Crosses Coloring
Keltic Alphabet Coloring: Capital Letters
Keltic Alphabet Coloring: Lower Case Letters
Keltic Coloring: Knots & Numbers

International Standard Book Number

ISBN-13: 978-1718680708
ISBN-10: 1718680708

www.ingramcontent.com/pod-product-compliance
Lightning Source LLC
Chambersburg PA
CBHW080045260726
48658CB00007B/2743